I Have Joy

IN MY HEART

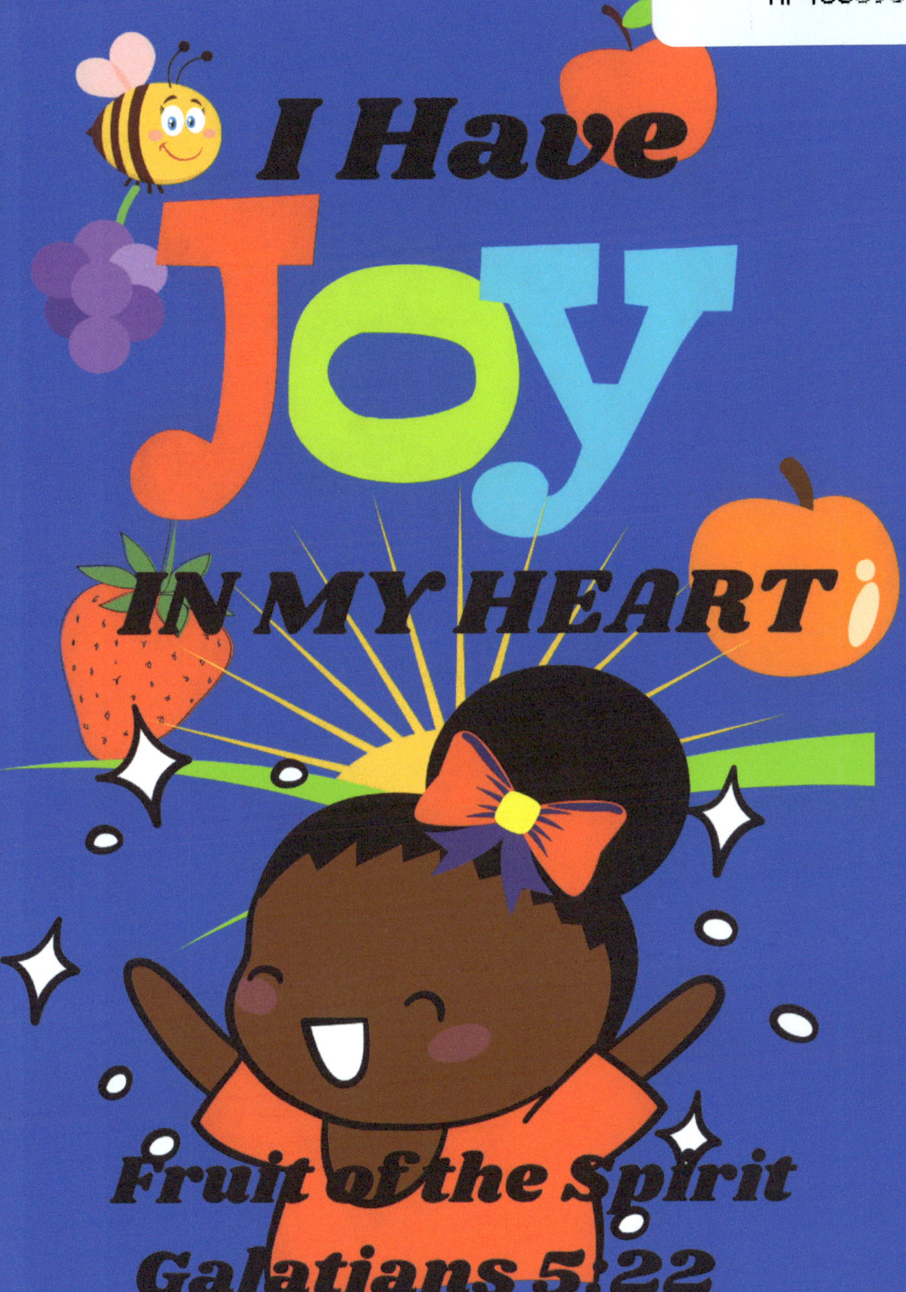

Fruit of the Spirit
Galatians 5:22

Denice Rohadfox

This Book
Belongs to

____

This is the day the Father has made and I will rejoice and be glad in it.
Psalm 118:24
JOY

I have joy in my heart when I am with my family.

I have joy in my heart when I play with my friends.

I have joy in my heart when we are blessed with food.

SOIL

I have joy
in my
heart
when I
visit my
favorite
place.

I have joy in my heart when I read my favorite book.

Plants
Genesis
1:29

I have joy
in my
heart
when I try
new
things.

I have joy
in my heart
when I
make new
friends .

READ

LIBRARY

OPEN
LIBRARY

I have joy in my heart when I am a good helper.

I have joy in my heart when I pray.

I have joy in my heart because I know my Heavenly Father

Loves me !

Do you have joy in your heart?

Did you know the Heavenly Father gives us joy?

How do you show your joy to others?

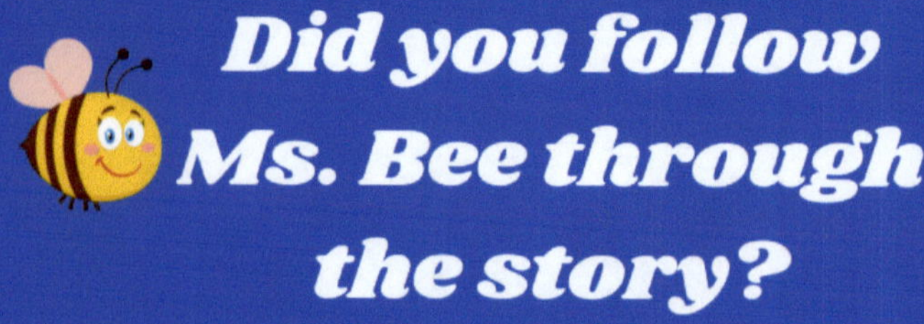
Did you follow Ms. Bee through the story?

Fruit of the Spirit

Galatians 5:22-23 - But the fruit of the Spirit is love, joy, peace, patience, kindness, goodness, faithfulness, gentleness, self-control; against such things there is no law

linktr.ee/childrenofthekingdom
Faith-Based Books for Children
https://www.amazon.com/author/denicebooks

Bye Bye

Joy